HAL•LEONARD®
EASY PIANO
PLAY-ALONG
AUDIO ACCESS INCLUDED

Disney's Best

Beauty and the Beast   2
BEAUTY AND THE BEAST

Bibbidi-Bobbidi-Boo   7
CINDERELLA

Chim Chim Cher-ee   10
MARY POPPINS

Colors of the Wind   22
POCAHONTAS

Friend Like Me   26
ALADDIN

Hakuna Matata   13
THE LION KING

Part of Your World   36
THE LITTLE MERMAID

Someday   42
THE HUNCHBACK OF NOTRE DAME

When She Loved Me   48
TOY STORY 2

You'll Be in My Heart   52
TARZAN™

T0079062

To access audio visit:
www.halleonard.com/mylibrary

1497-6681-1216-1486

ISBN 978-0-4234-0138-4

Wonderland Music Company, Inc. Walt Disney Music Company

DISTRIBUTED BY

HAL•LEONARD®
CORPORATION
7777 W. BLUEMOUND RD. P.O. BOX 13819 MILWAUKEE, WI 53213

In Australia Contact:
Hal Leonard Australia Pty. Ltd.
4 Lentara Court
Cheltenham, Victoria, 3192 Australia
Email: ausadmin@halleonard.com

Visit Hal Leonard Online at **www.halleonard.com**

BEAUTY AND THE BEAST

from Walt Disney's BEAUTY AND THE BEAST

Lyrics by HOWARD ASHMAN
Music by ALAN MENKEN

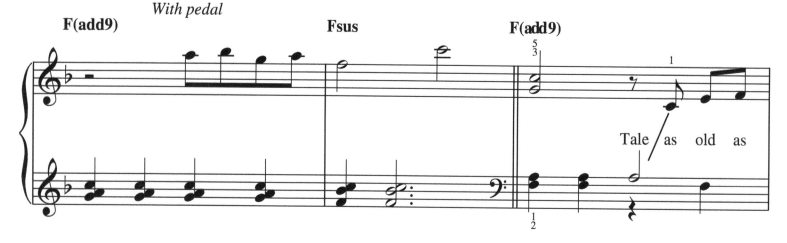

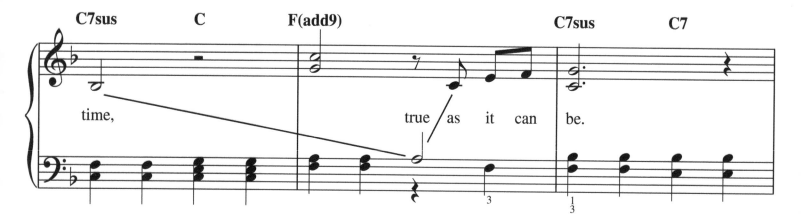

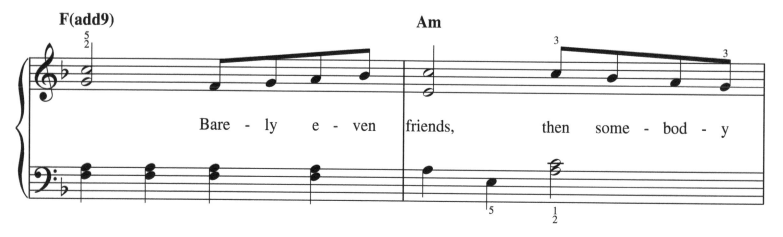

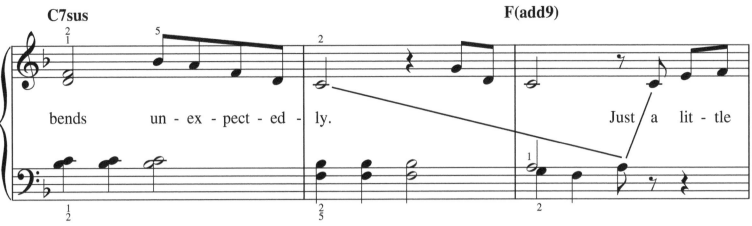

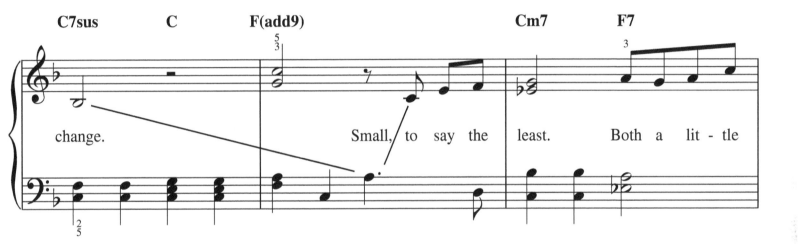

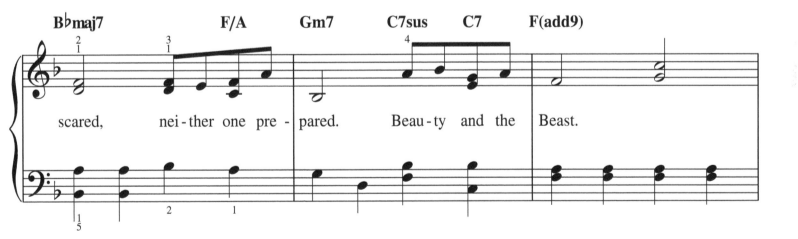

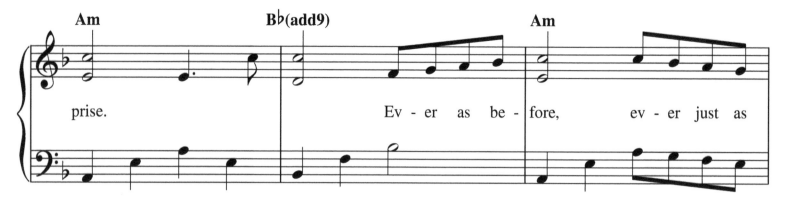

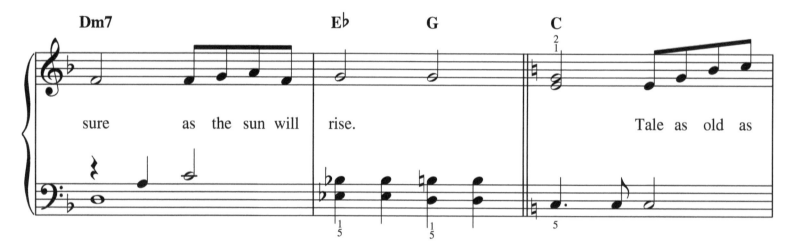

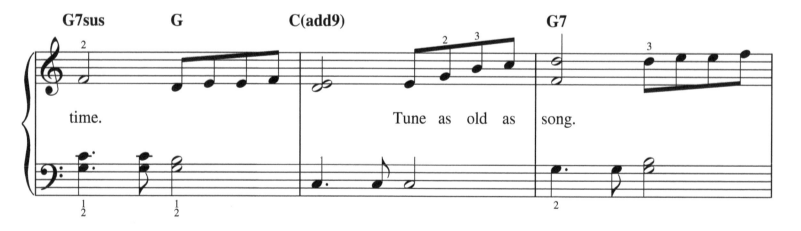

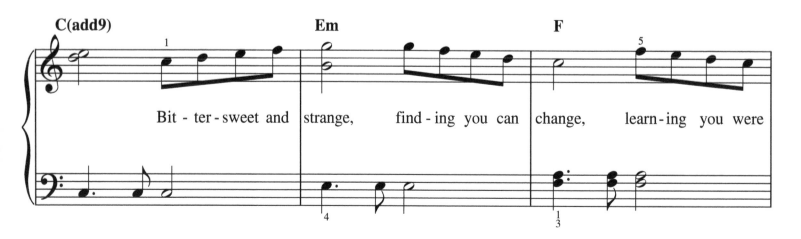

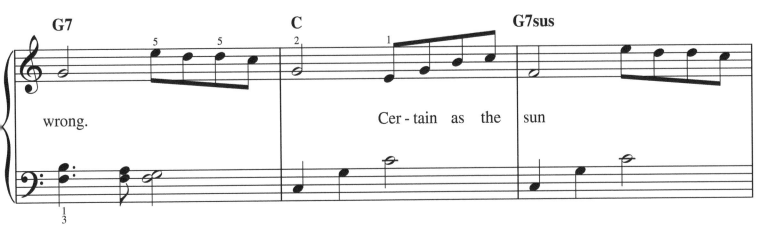

wrong. Cer - tain as the sun rising in the East.

ris - ing in the East. Tale as old as time, song as old as

rhyme. Beau - ty and the Beast.

rit. a tempo

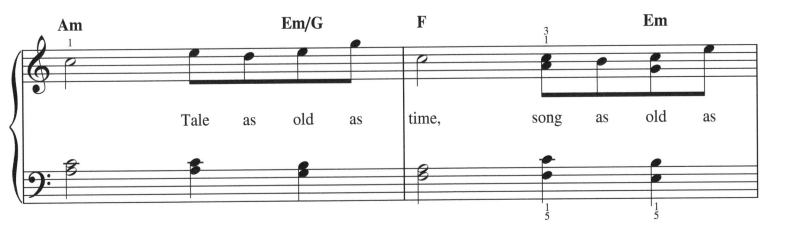

Tale as old as time, song as old as

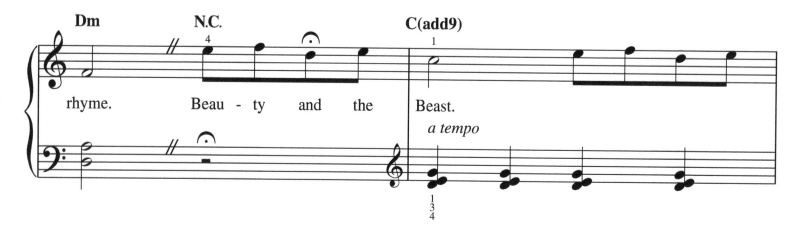

rhyme.   Beau - ty   and   the   Beast.

a tempo

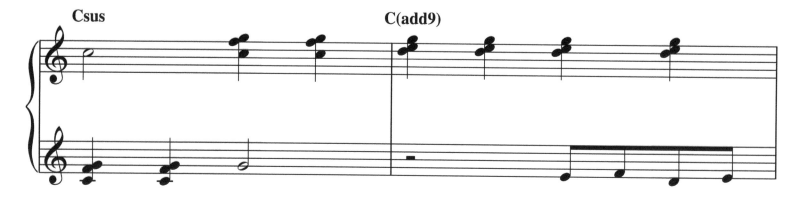

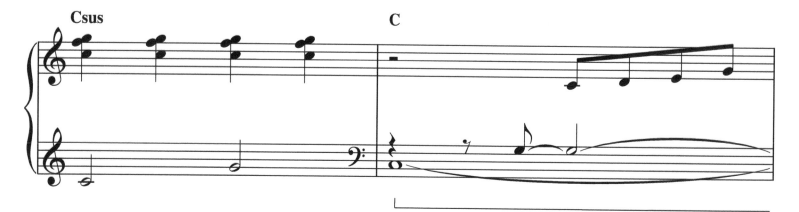

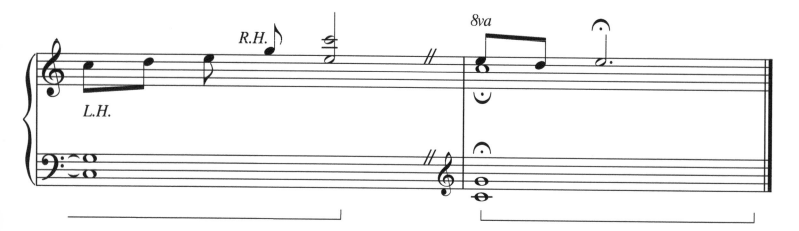

BIBBIDI-BOBBIDI-BOO
(The Magic Song)
from Walt Disney's CINDERELLA

Words by JERRY LIVINGSTON
Music by MACK DAVID and AL HOFFMAN

Sa - la - ga - doo - la men - chic - ka boo - la bib - bi - di - bob - bi - di - boo.

Put 'em to - geth - er and what have you got? Bib - bi - di - bob - bi - di - boo.

Sa - la - ga - doo - la men - chic - ka boo - la bib - bi - di - bob - bi - di - boo.

Put 'em to - geth - er and what have you got? Bib - bi - di - bob - bi - di - boo.

Bib - bi - di - bob - bi - di, bib - bi - di - bob - bi - di, bib - bi - di - bob - bi - di - boo.

CHIM CHIM CHER-EE

from Walt Disney's MARY POPPINS

Words and Music by RICHARD M. SHERMAN
and ROBERT B. SHERMAN

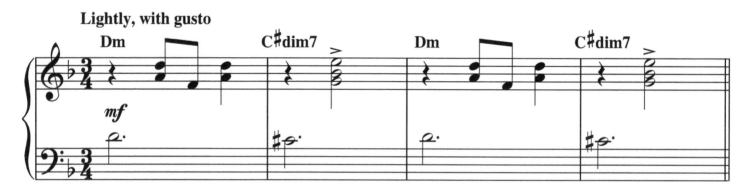

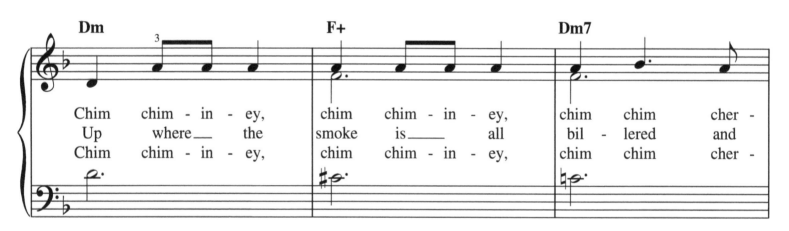

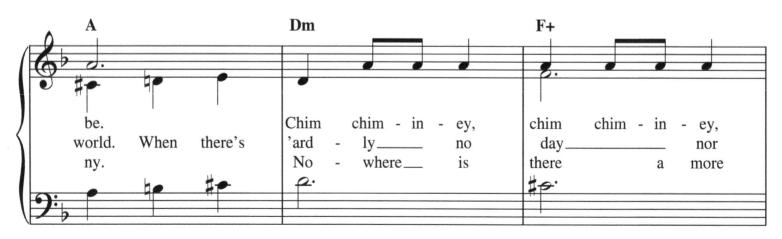

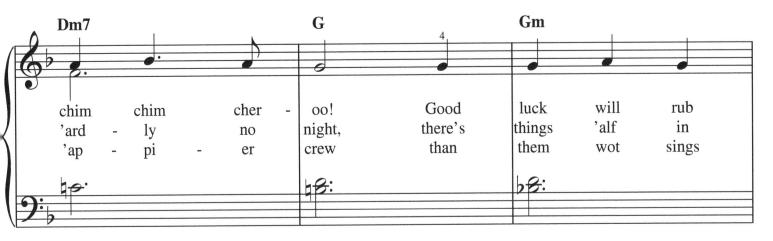

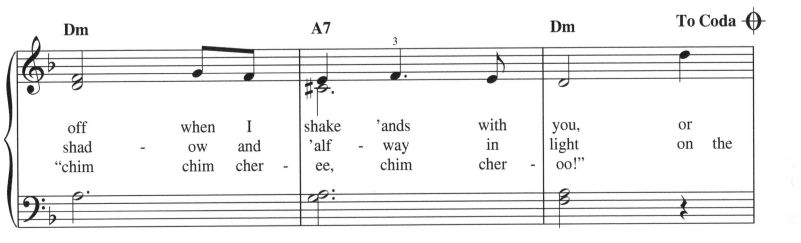

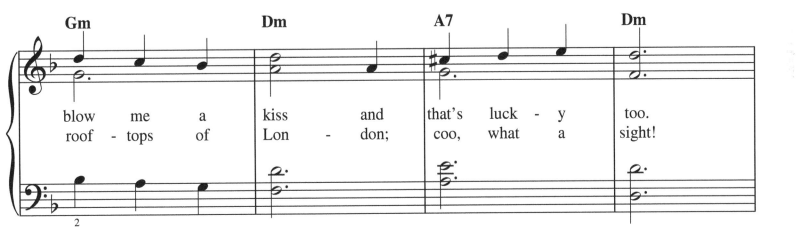

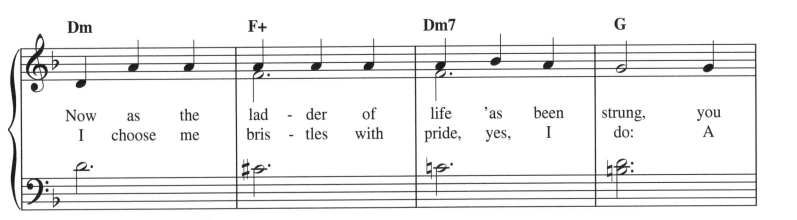

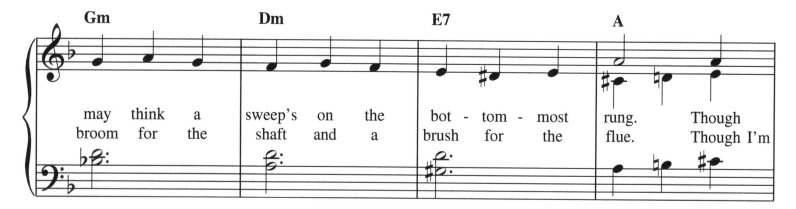

may think a / broom for the

sweep's on the / shaft and a

bot - tom - most / brush for the

rung. Though / flue. Though I'm

I spends me / cov - ered with

time in the / soot from me

ash - es and / 'ead to me

smoke, in / toes, a

1st time: D.C.
2nd time: D.C. al Coda

this 'ole wide / sweep knows 'e's

world there's no / wel - come wher -

'ap - pi - er / ev - er 'e

bloke. / goes.

CODA

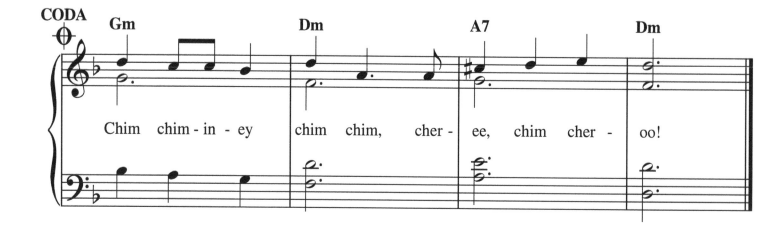

Chim chim - in - ey

chim chim, cher - ee,

chim cher -

oo!

HAKUNA MATATA

from Walt Disney Pictures' THE LION KING

Music by ELTON JOHN
Lyrics by TIM RICE

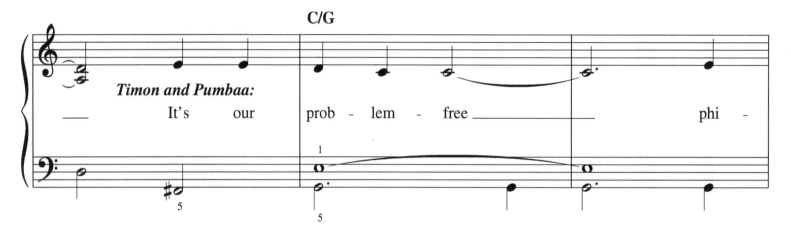

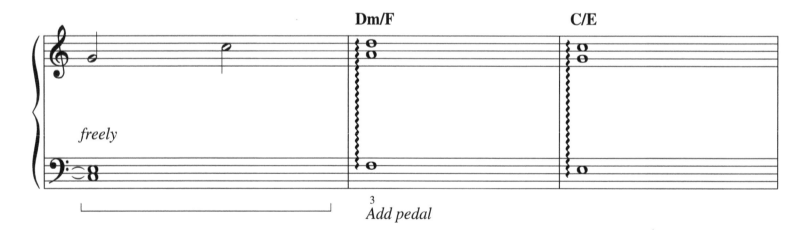

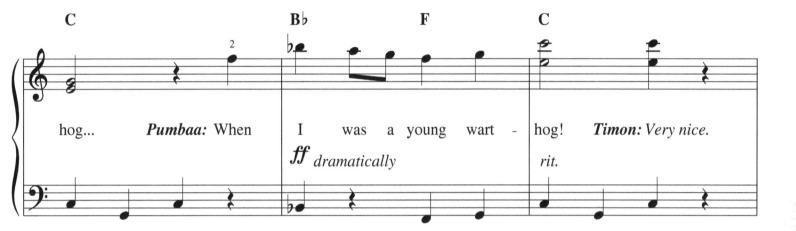

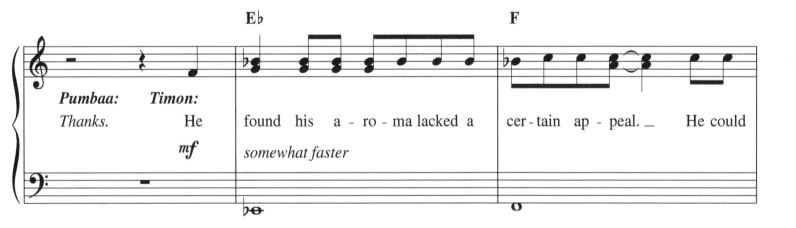

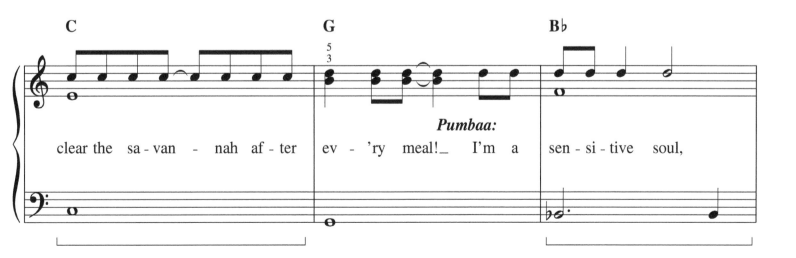

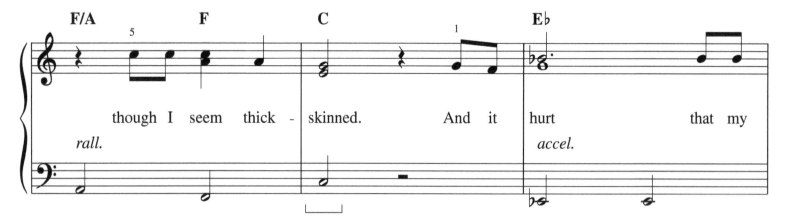

though I seem thick - skinned. And it hurt that my
rall. *accel.*

friends nev - er stood down - wind!
(Spoken:) And, oh, ___ the
rit.

Timon:
shame! He was a -
Pumbaa:
shamed! Thought of chang-in' my
Timon:
name! Oh, what's in a
a tempo

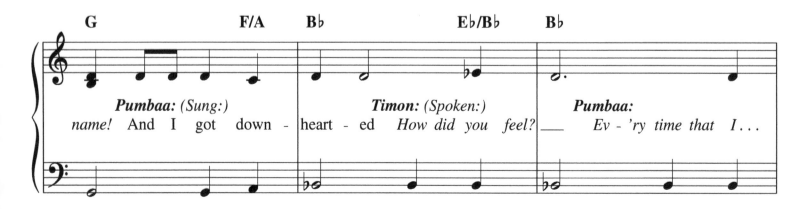

Pumbaa: *(Sung:)*
name! And I got down - heart - ed
Timon: *(Spoken:)*
How did you feel? ___
Pumbaa:
Ev - 'ry time that I...

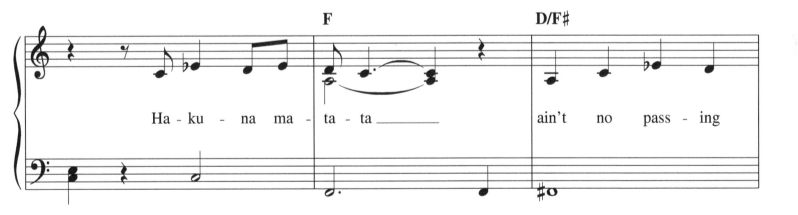

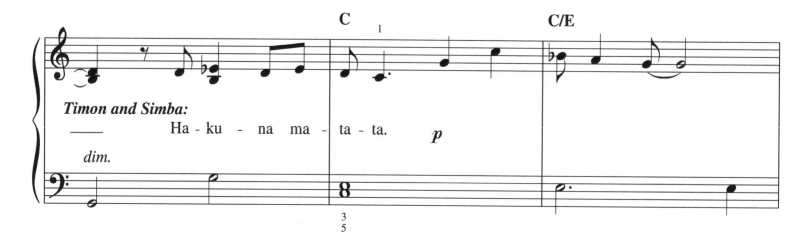

All: (Spoken:) Hakuna matata. cresc. poco a poco Hakuna matata.

Add pedal

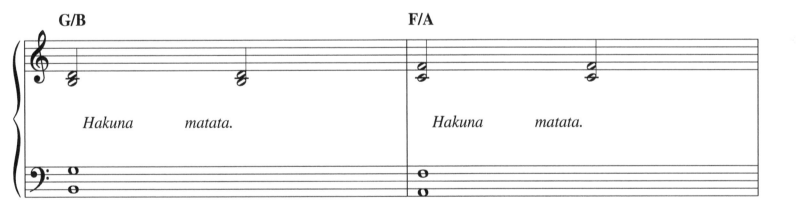

Hakuna matata. Hakuna matata.

Hakuna matata. Hakuna matata.

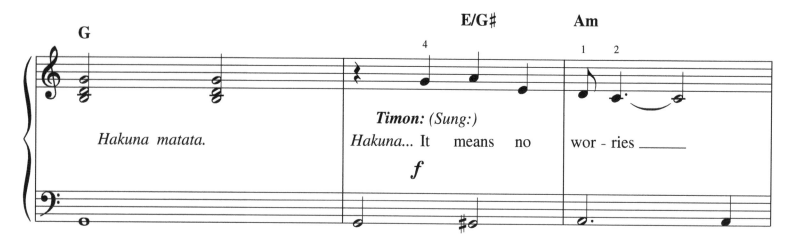

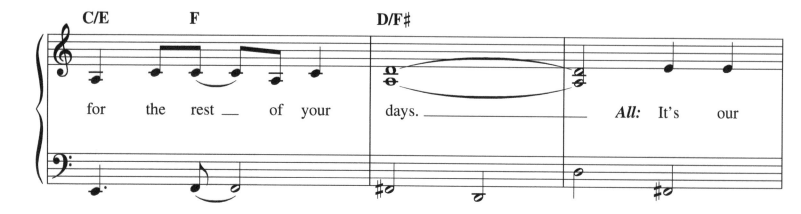

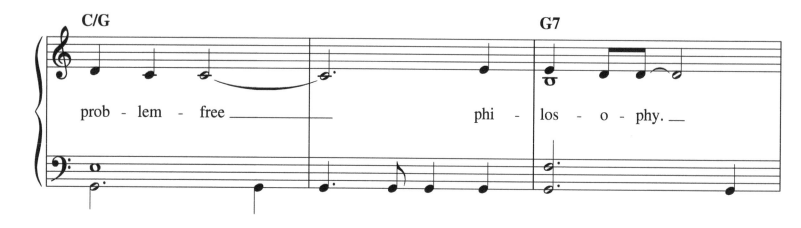

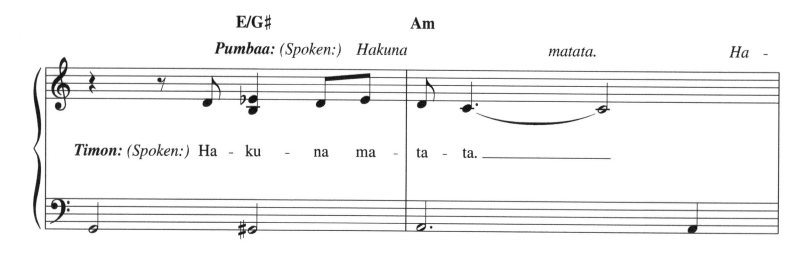

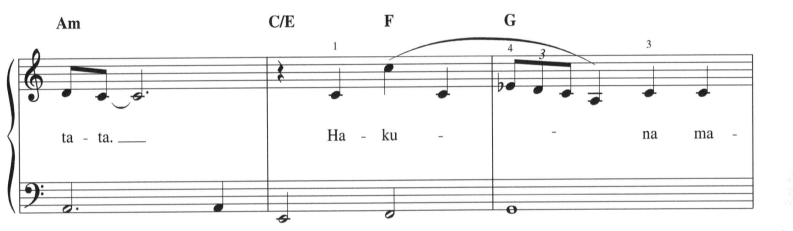

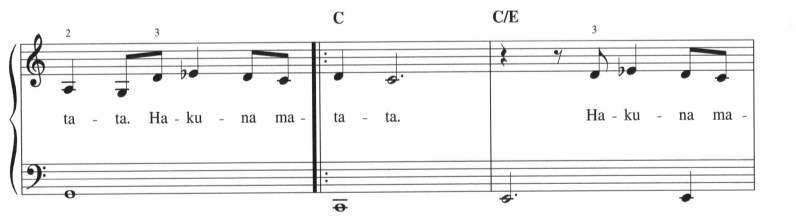

COLORS OF THE WIND

from Walt Disney's POCAHONTAS

Music by ALAN MENKEN
Lyrics by STEPHEN SCHWARTZ

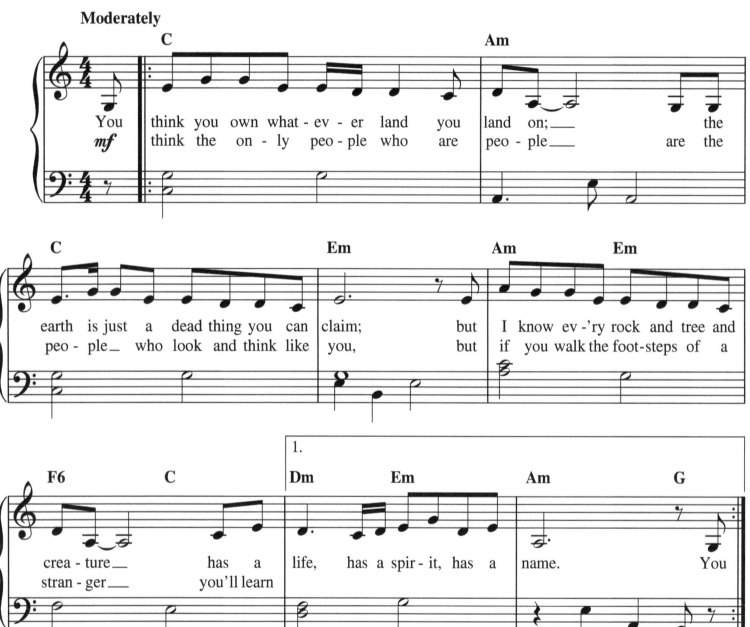

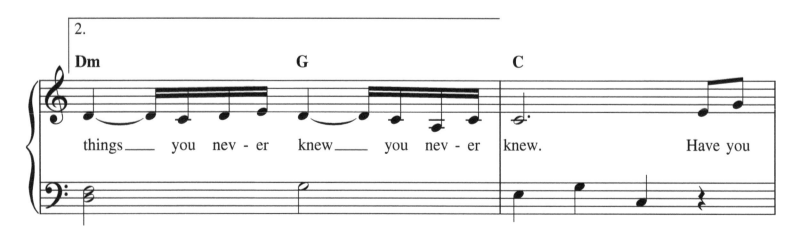

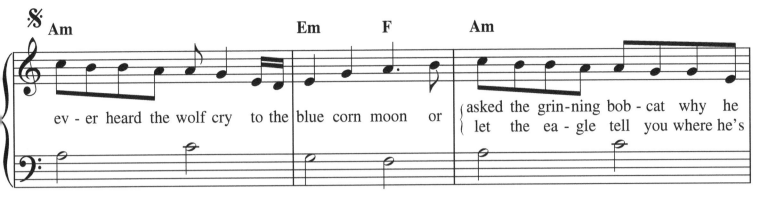

ev - er heard the wolf cry to the blue corn moon or
asked the grin-ning bob - cat why he
let the ea - gle tell you where he's

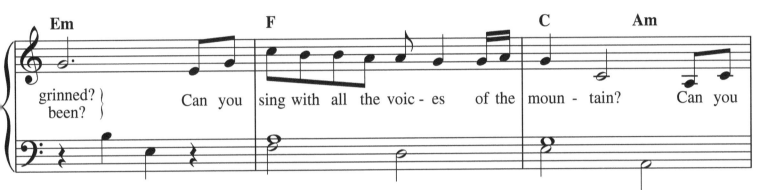

grinned?
been?
Can you sing with all the voic - es of the moun - tain? Can you

paint with all the col -ors of the wind? Can you paint with all the col -ors of the

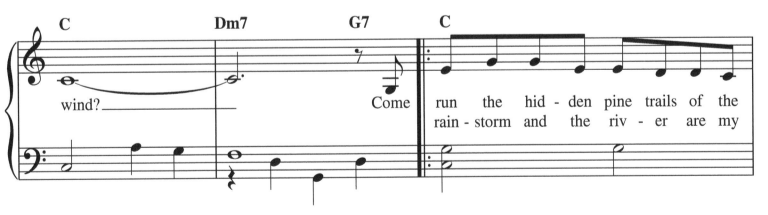

wind?_____ Come run the hid - den pine trails of the
rain - storm and the riv - er are my

for - est,____
broth - ers:____
come
the
taste the sun - sweet ber - ries of the
her - on and the ot - ter are my

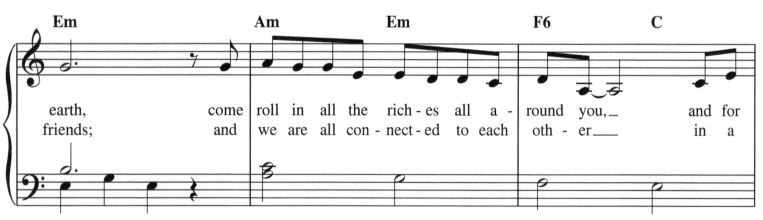

Em   **Am**   **Em**   **F6**   **C**

earth,   come roll in all the rich - es all a - round you,__ and for

friends;   and we are all con - nect - ed to each oth - er__ in a

1. **Dm**   **Em**   **Am**   **G**   2. **Dm**   **Dm/G**

once nev - er won - der what they're worth. The cir - cle, in a hoop that

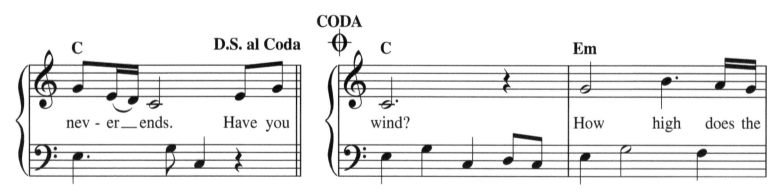

C   **D.S. al Coda**   **CODA**   **C**   **Em**

nev - er__ ends. Have you   wind?   How high does the

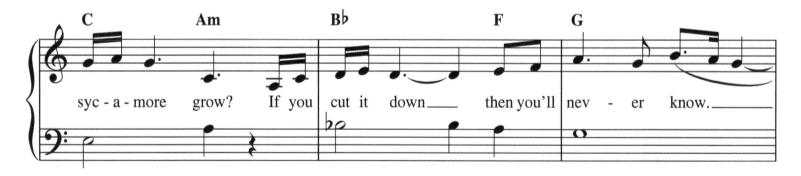

C   **Am**   **B♭**   **F**   **G**

syc - a - more grow? If you cut it down__ then you'll nev - er know.__

Dm   **Am**   **Em**   **F**

__ And you'll nev - er hear the wolf cry to the blue corn moon, for

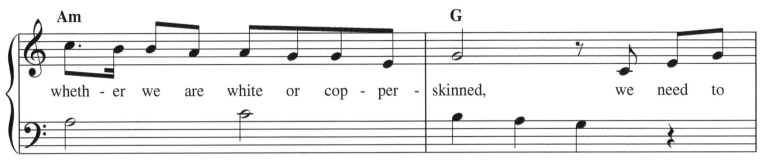

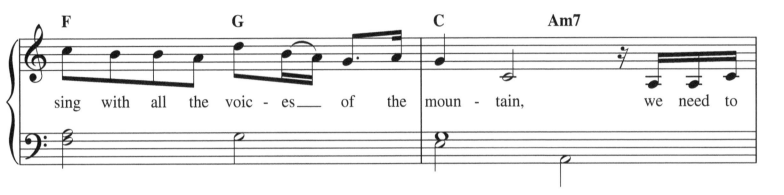

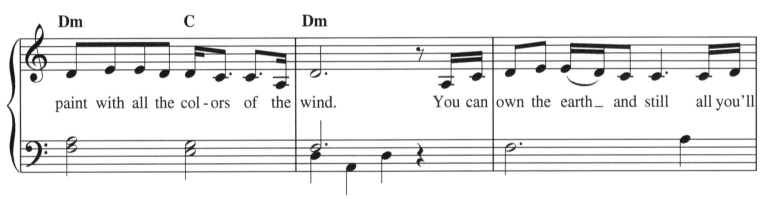

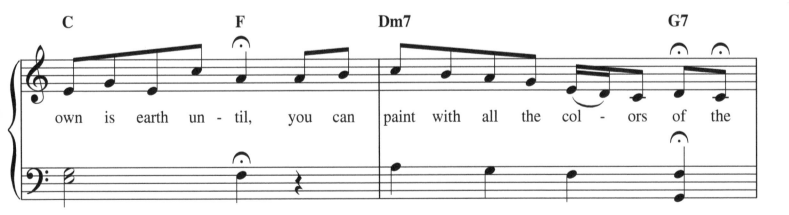

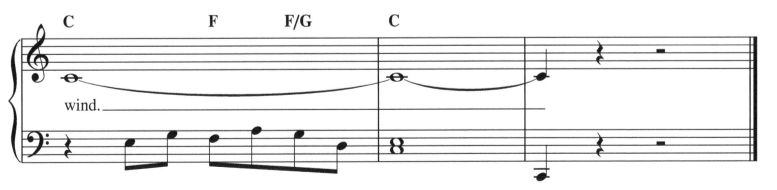

FRIEND LIKE ME
from Walt Disney's ALADDIN

Lyrics by HOWARD ASHMAN
Music by ALAN MENKEN

Moderately bright

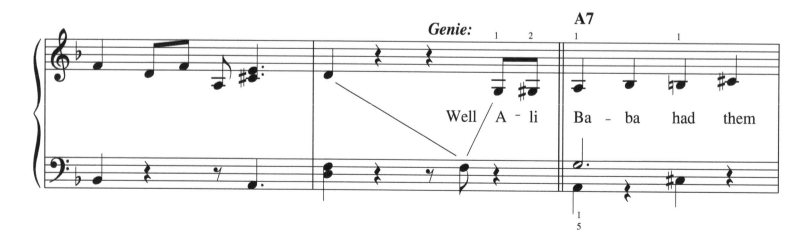

Genie:

Well A - li Ba - ba had them

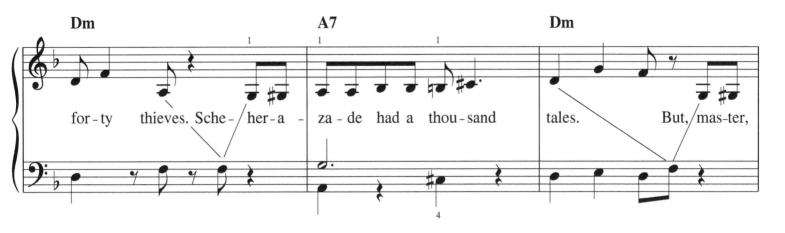

for-ty thieves. Sche - her-a - za - de had a thou-sand tales. But, mas-ter,

you in luck 'cause up your sleeves _ you got a brand of mag-ic nev-er

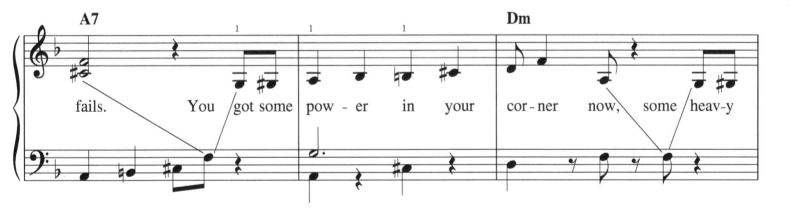

fails. You got some pow - er in your cor-ner now, some heav-y

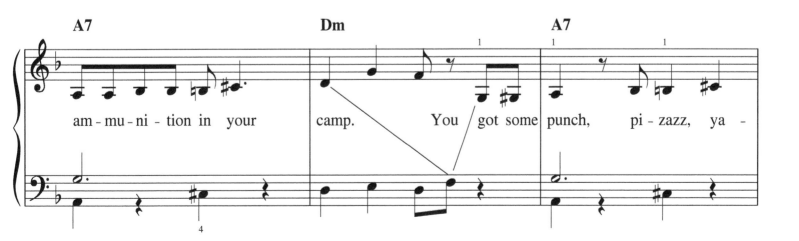

am-mu-ni-tion in your camp. You got some punch, pi-zazz, ya -

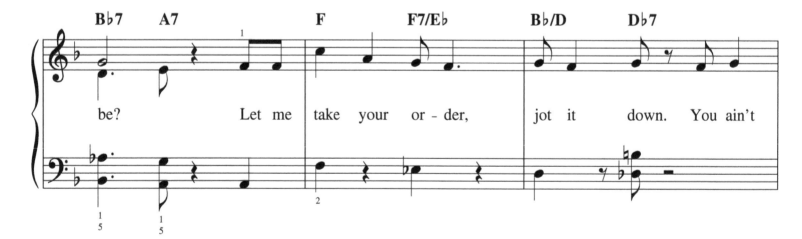

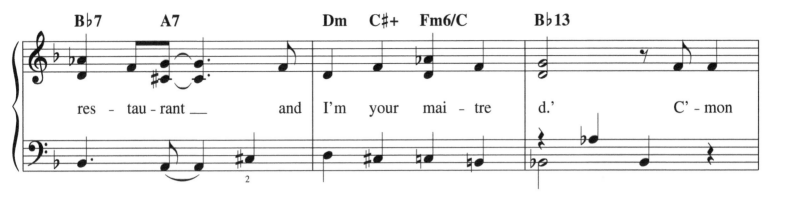

res - tau - rant ___ and I'm your mai - tre d.' C' - mon

whis - per what it is you want. You ain't nev - er had a friend like

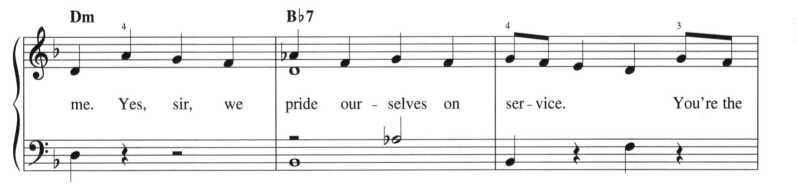

me. Yes, sir, we pride our - selves on ser - vice. You're the

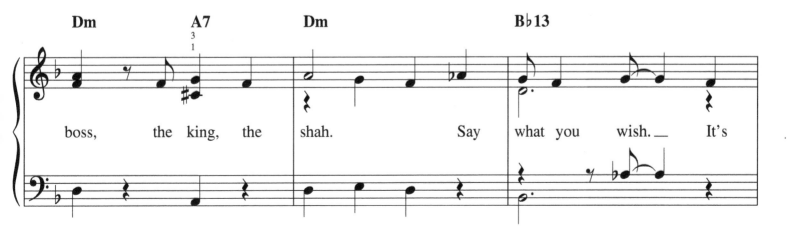

boss, the king, the shah. Say what you wish. ___ It's

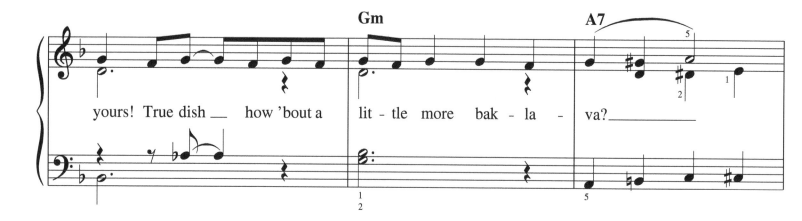

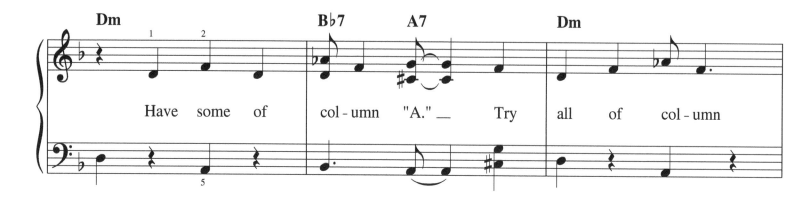

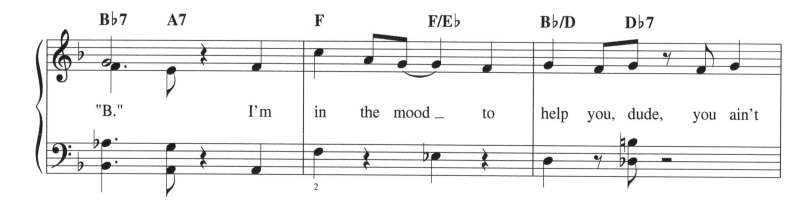

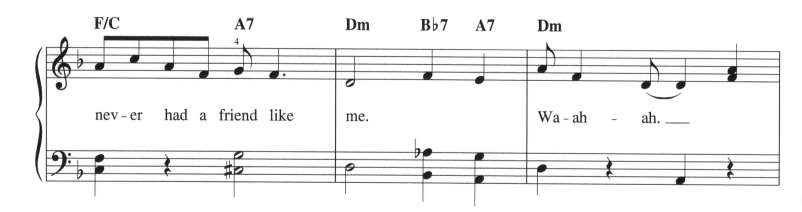

Oh my. Wa-ah - ah. No no.

Wa-ah - ah. Na na na.

Can your friends do this? Can your friends do

that? Can your friends pull this

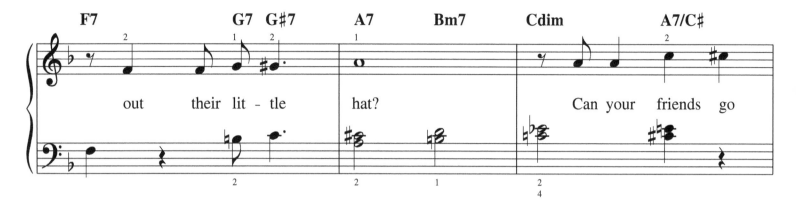

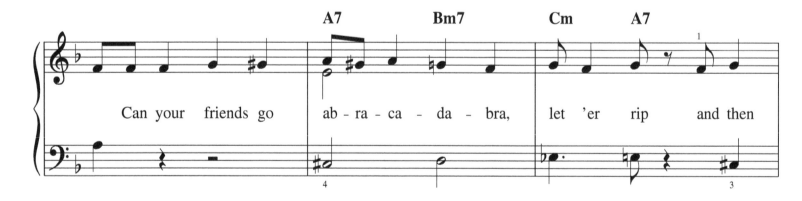

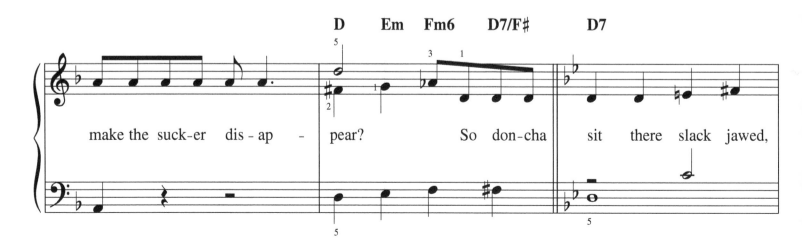

bug-gy eyed. I'm here to an-swer all your mid-day prayers. You got me

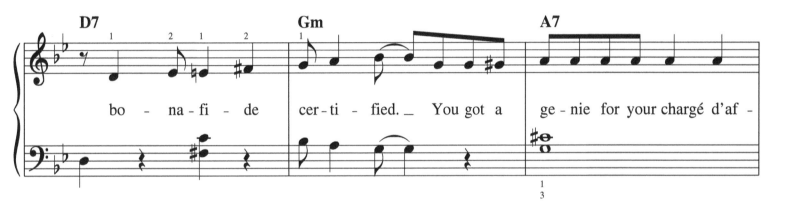

bo - na - fi - de cer - ti - fied. _ You got a ge - nie for your chargé d'af -

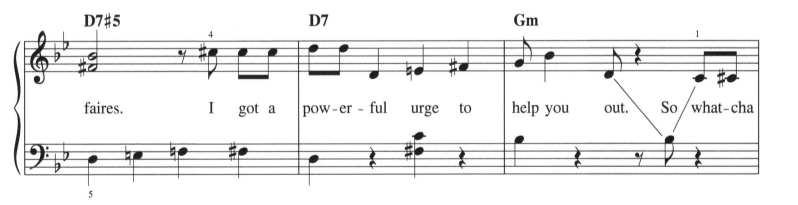

faires. I got a pow-er-ful urge to help you out. So what-cha

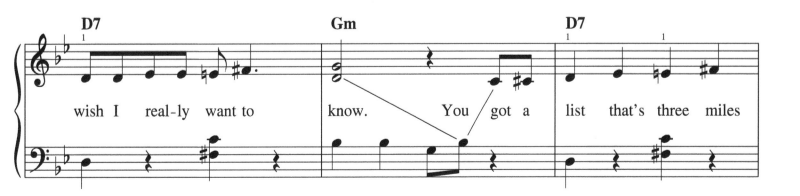

wish I real-ly want to know. You got a list that's three miles

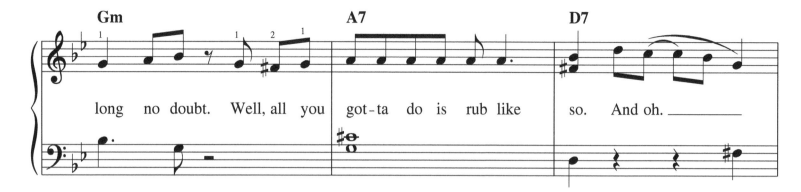

long no doubt. Well, all you got-ta do is rub like so. And oh. _____

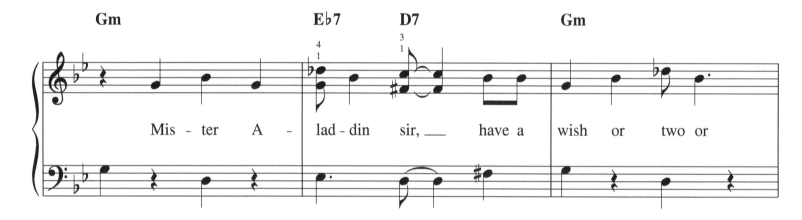

Mis - ter A - lad-din sir, ___ have a wish or two or

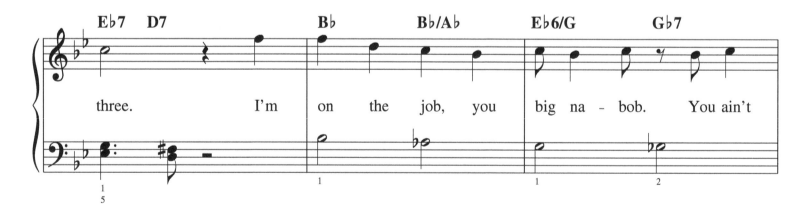

three. I'm on the job, you big na - bob. You ain't

nev-er had a friend, nev-er had a friend, you ain't nev-er had a friend, nev-er

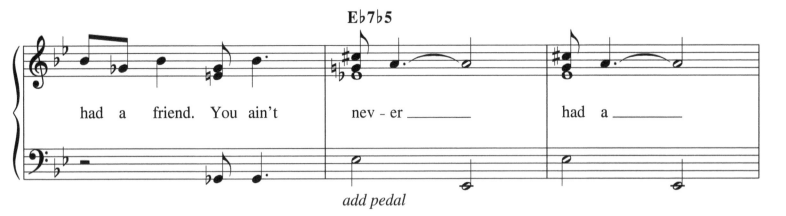

had a   friend. You ain't   nev-er _____   had a _____

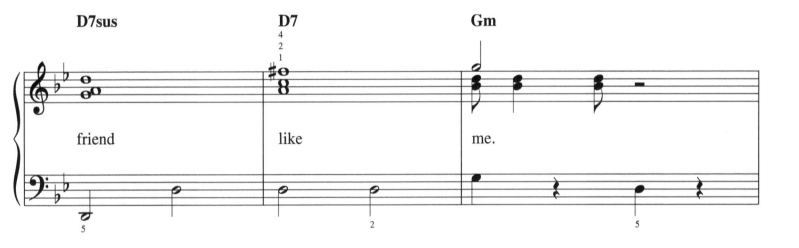

friend   like   me.

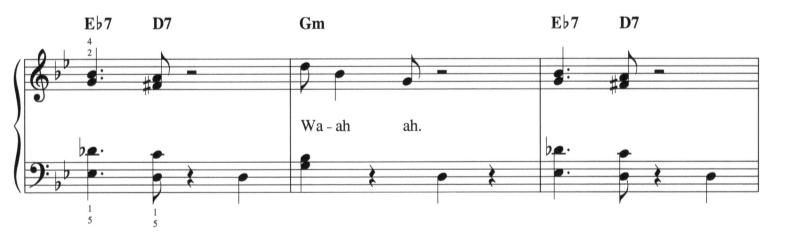

Wa - ah   ah.

Wa ah   ah.   You ain't   nev-er had a friend like   me.   Ha!

PART OF YOUR WORLD

from Walt Disney's THE LITTLE MERMAID

Lyrics by HOWARD ASHMAN
Music by ALAN MENKEN

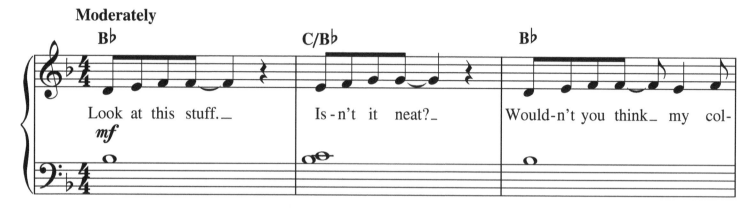

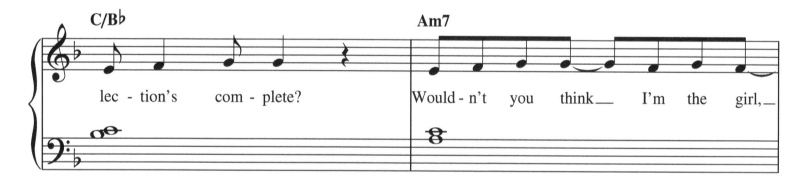

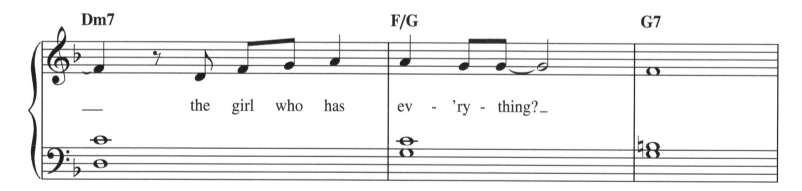

one cav - ern hold? Look - ing a - round__ here you'd think__ sure, she's got

ev - 'ry - thing.__ I've got gad - gets and giz - mos a -

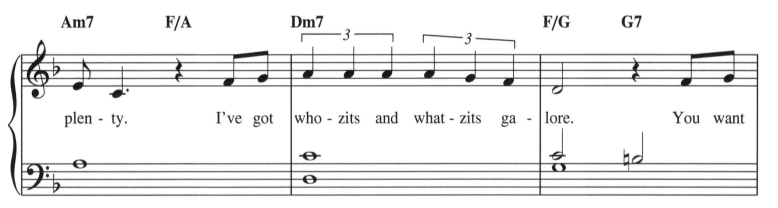

plen - ty. I've got who - zits and what - zits ga - lore. You want

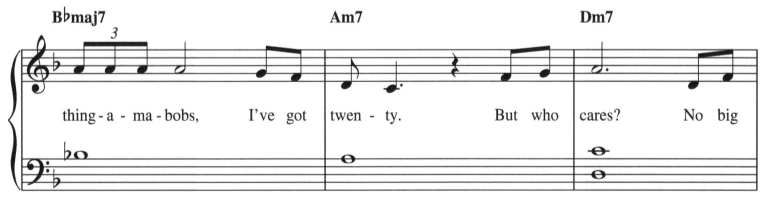

thing - a - ma - bobs, I've got twen - ty. But who cares? No big

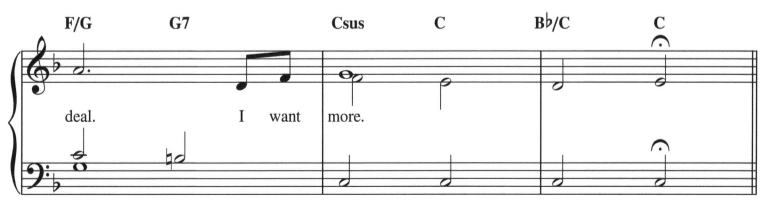

deal. I want more.

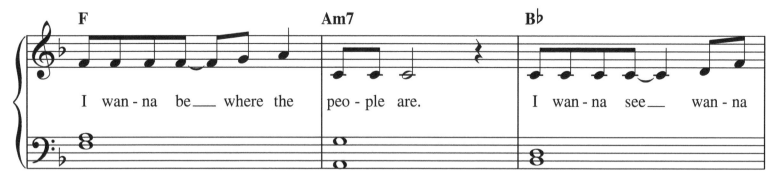

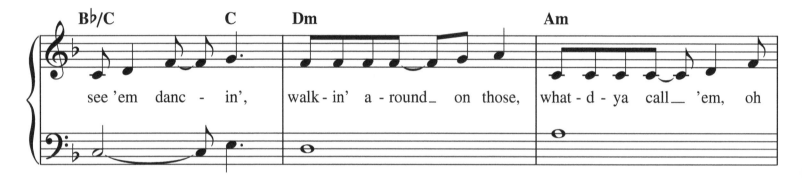

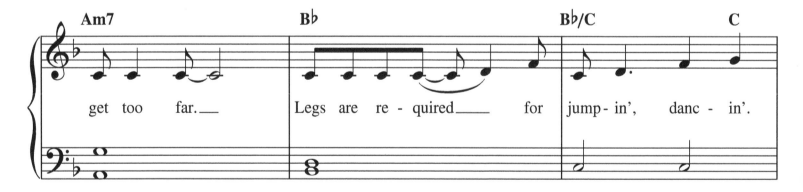

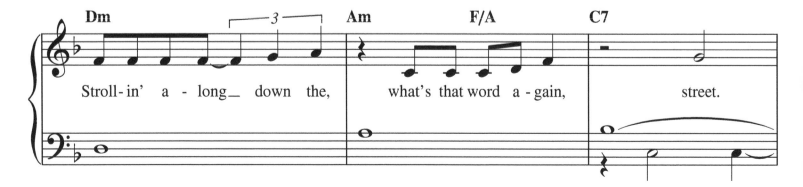

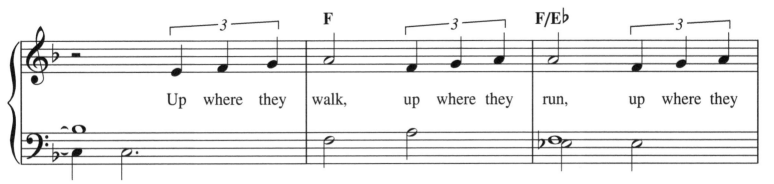

Up where they walk, up where they run, up where they

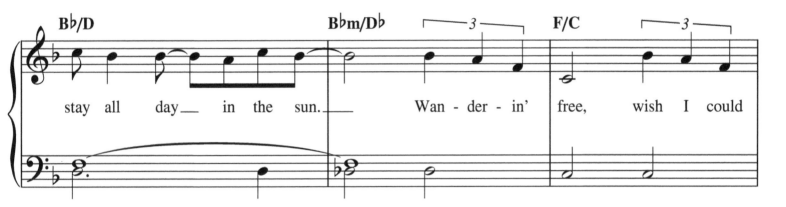

stay all day___ in the sun.___ Wan - der - in' free, wish I could

be part of that world._____ What would I

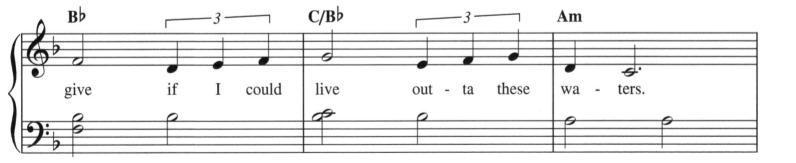

give if I could live out - ta these wa - ters.

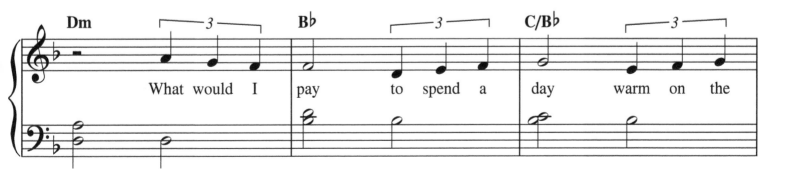

What would I pay to spend a day warm on the

40

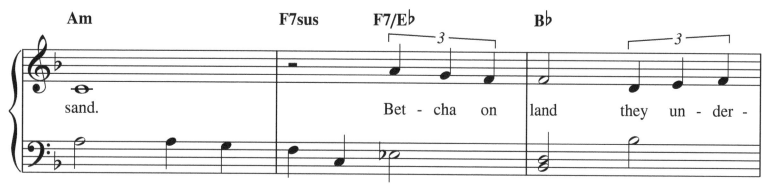

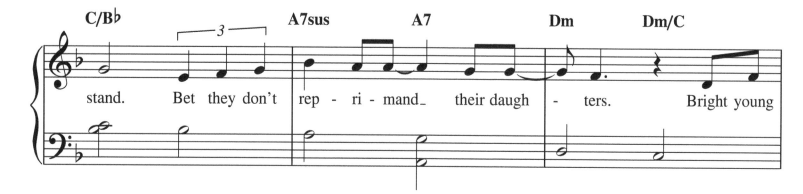

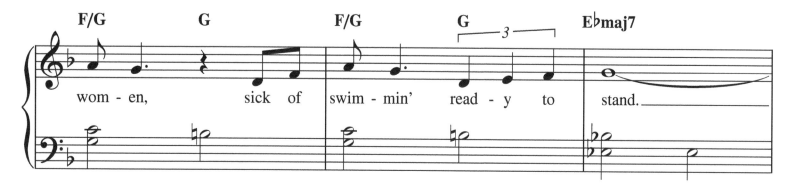

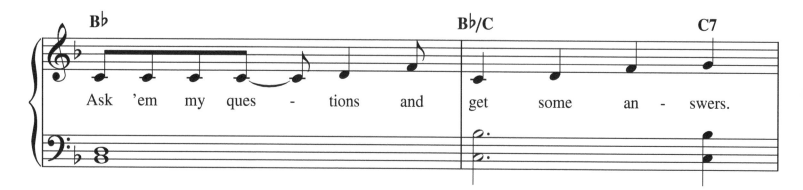

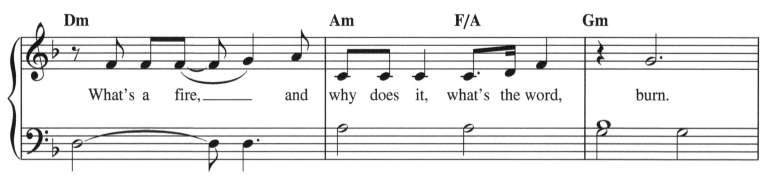

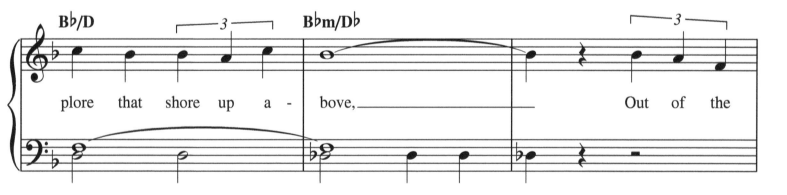

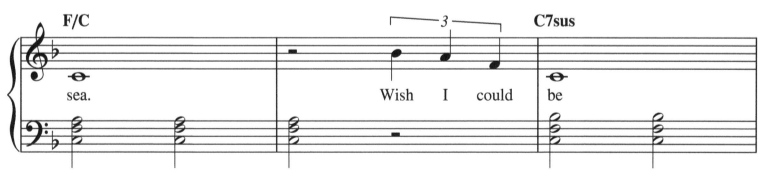

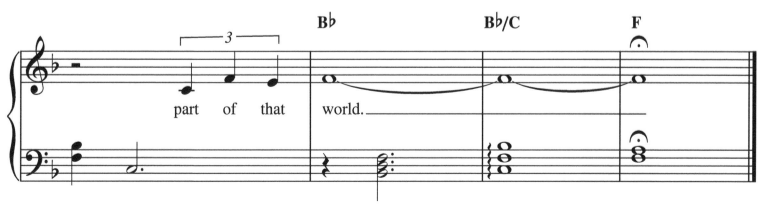

SOMEDAY

from Walt Disney's THE HUNCHBACK OF NOTRE DAME

Music by ALAN MENKEN
Lyrics by STEPHEN SCHWARTZ

Gently

mp

With pedal

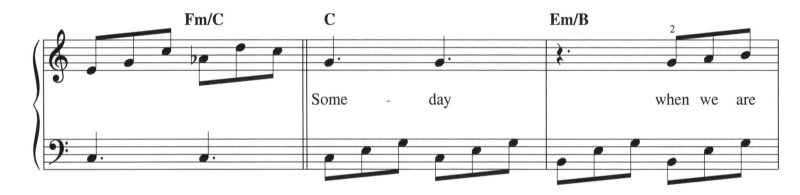

Some - day when we are

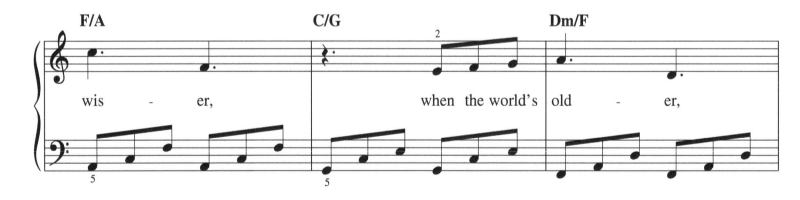

wis - er, when the world's old - er,

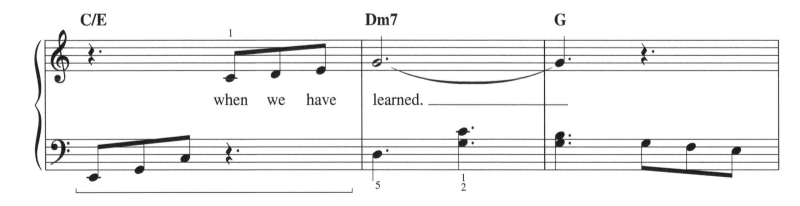

when we have learned.

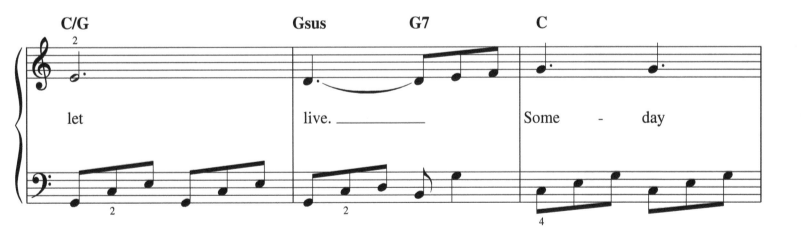

44

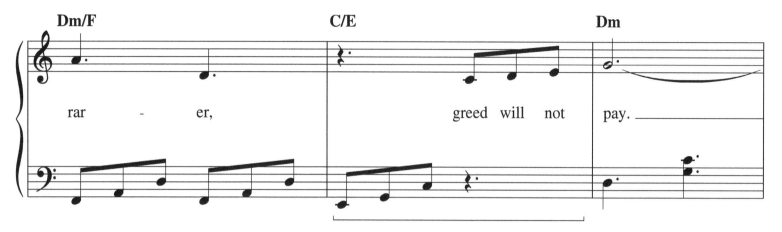

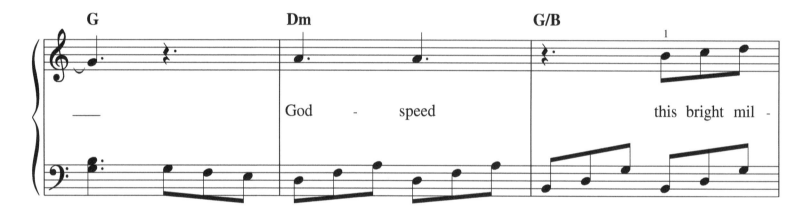

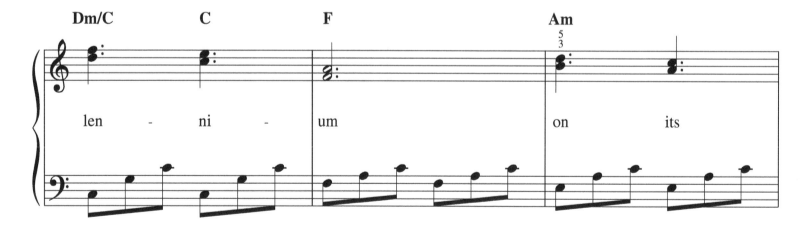

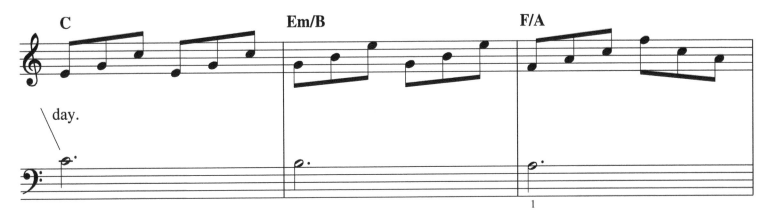

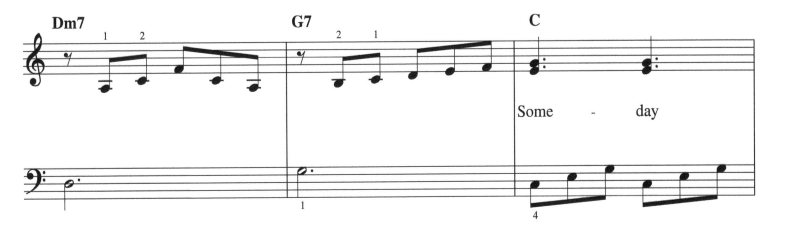

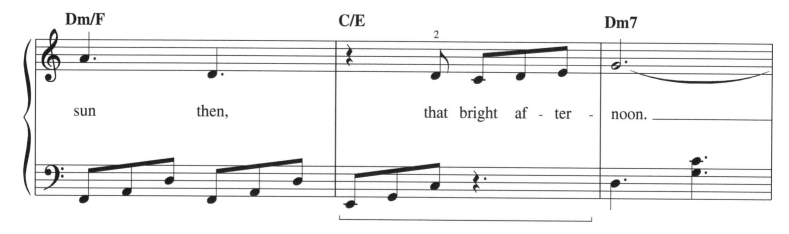

sun then, that bright af - ter - noon. ____

____ Till then, on days when the

sun is gone, we'll hang

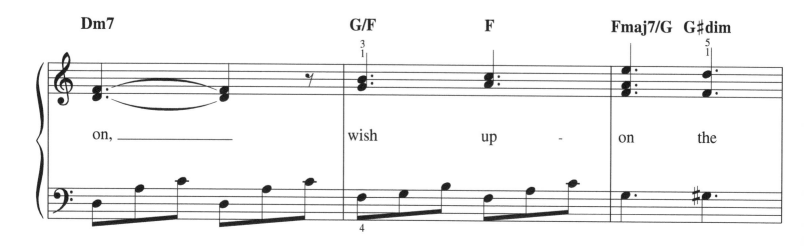

on, ____ wish up - on the

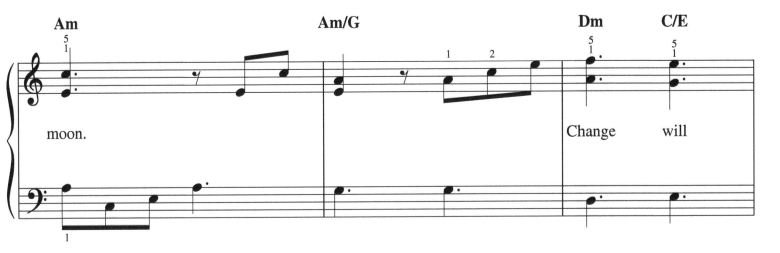

moon.

Change will

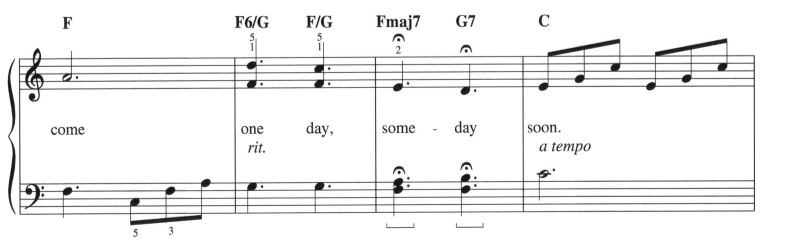

come

one day,

rit.

some - day

soon.

a tempo

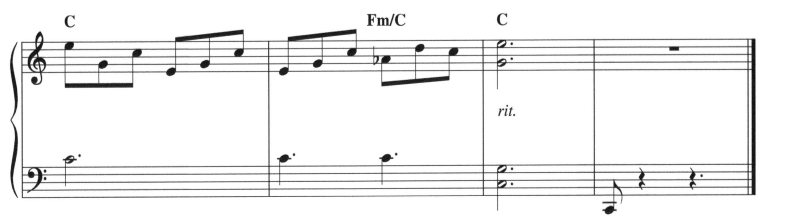

rit.

WHEN SHE LOVED ME

from Walt Disney Pictures' TOY STORY 2 - A Pixar Film

Music and Lyrics by
RANDY NEWMAN

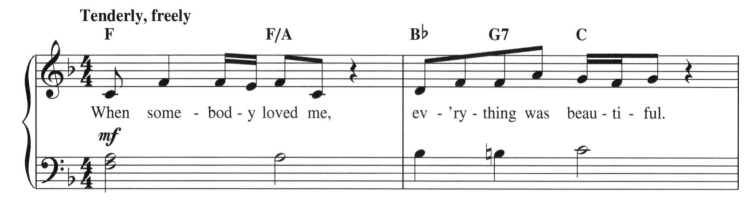

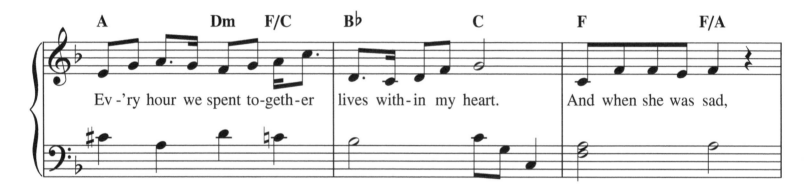

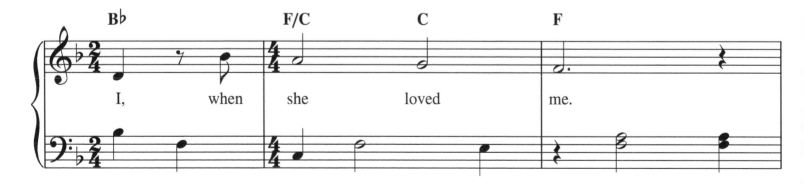

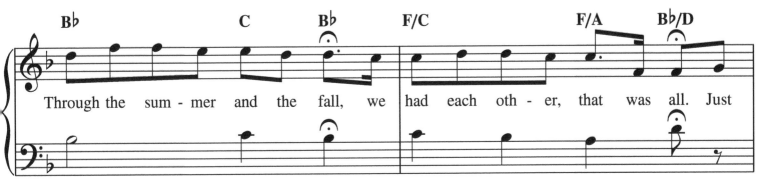

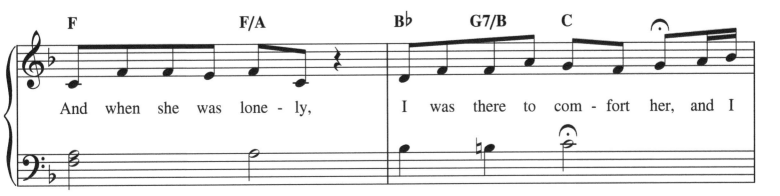

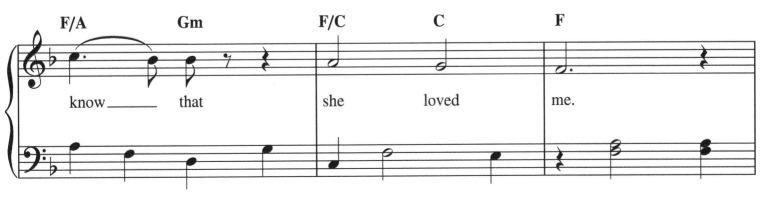

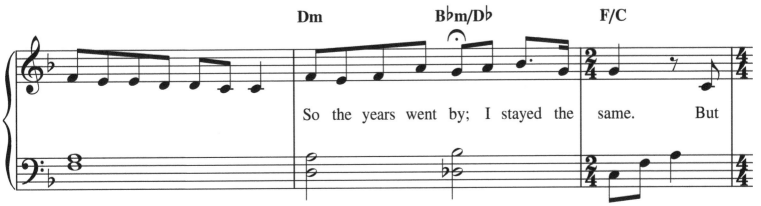

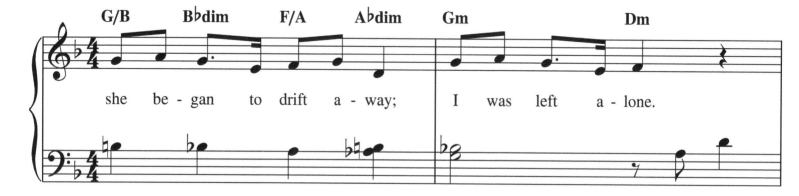

she be-gan to drift a-way; I was left a-lone.

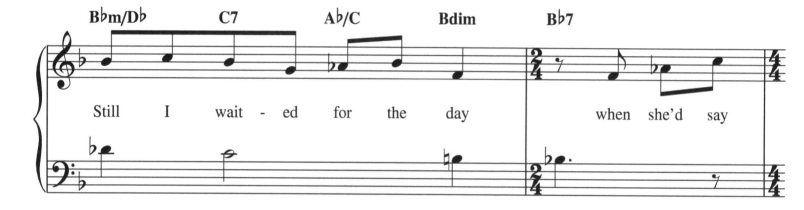

Still I wait-ed for the day when she'd say

"I will al-ways love you." Lone-ly and for-got-ten,

nev-er thought she'd look my way, and she smiled at me and held me just

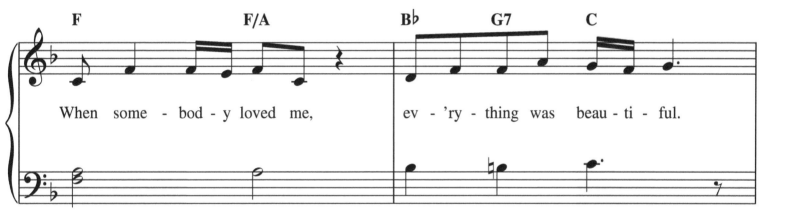

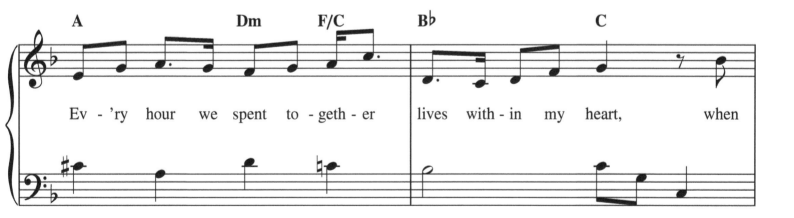

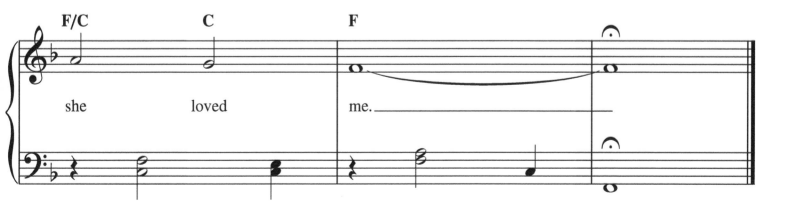

YOU'LL BE IN MY HEART

from Walt Disney Pictures' TARZAN ™

Words and Music by
PHIL COLLINS

Moderately

Come stop your cry-ing; it-'ll be all right.

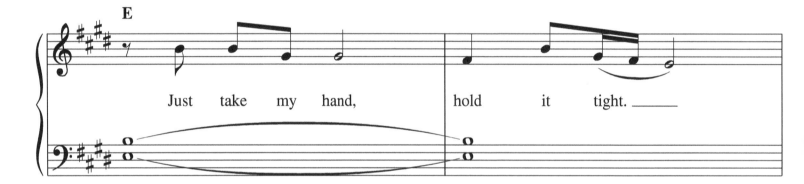

Just take my hand, hold it tight.

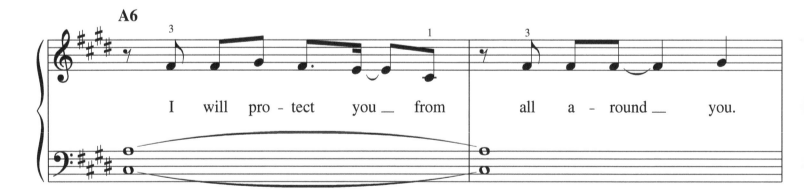

I will pro-tect you ___ from all a-round ___ you.

I will be here, don't you cry. For one so small you

seem so strong. __ My arms will hold you, keep you safe and warm. __

This bond be-tween us can't be bro - ken. I will be here; don't you

cry. 'Cause you'll be in my heart, yes,

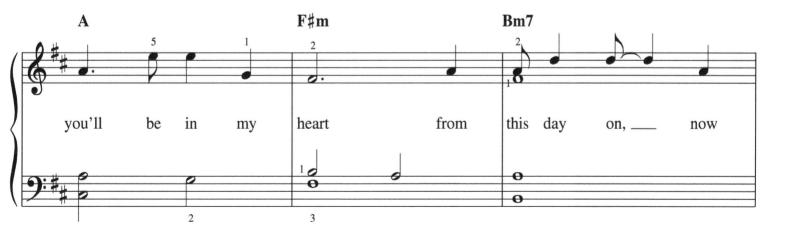

you'll be in my heart from this day on, ___ now

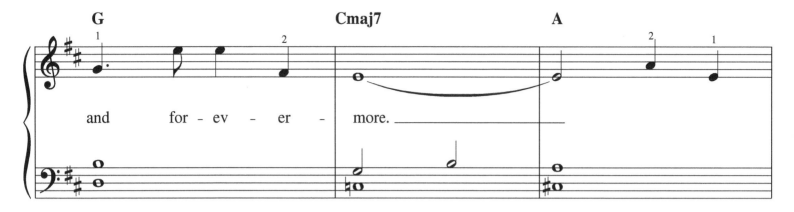

and for - ev - er - more. _____

You'll be in my heart no mat - ter what __ they

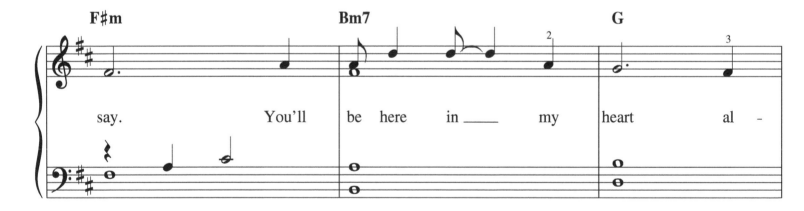

say. You'll be here in _____ my heart al -

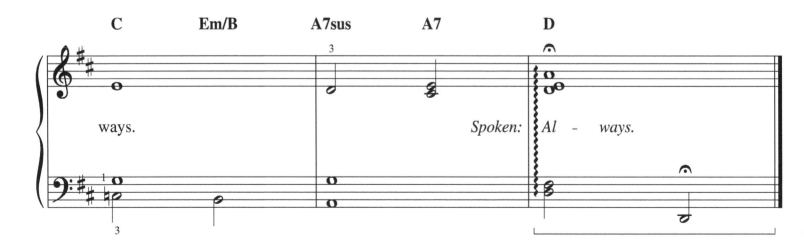

ways. *Spoken:* Al - ways.

EASY PIANO PLAY-ALONGS
Orchestrated arrangements with you as the soloist!

This series lets you play along with great accompaniments to songs you know and love! Each book comes with recordings of complete professional performances and includes matching custom arrangements in easy piano format. With these books you can: Listen to complete professional performances of each of the songs; Play the easy piano arrangements along with the performances; Sing along with the recordings; Play the easy piano arrangements as solos, without the audio.

1. GREAT JAZZ STANDARDS
00310916 Book/CD Pack......................$14.95

2. FAVORITE CLASSICAL THEMES
00310921 Book/CD Pack......................$14.95

3. BROADWAY FAVORITES
00310915 Book/CD Pack......................$14.95

4. ADELE
00156223 Book/Online Audio................$16.99

5. HIT POP/ROCK BALLADS
00310917 Book/CD Pack......................$14.95

6. LOVE SONG FAVORITES
00310918 Book/CD Pack......................$14.95

7. O HOLY NIGHT
00310920 Book/CD Pack......................$14.95

9. COUNTRY BALLADS
00311105 Book/CD Pack......................$14.95

11. DISNEY BLOCKBUSTERS
00311107 Book/Online Audio................$14.99

12. CHRISTMAS FAVORITES
00311257 Book/CD Pack......................$14.95

13. CHILDREN'S SONGS
00311258 Book/CD Pack......................$14.95

15. DISNEY'S BEST
00311260 Book/Online Audio...............$16.99

16. LENNON & McCARTNEY HITS
00311262 Book/CD Pack......................$14.95

17. HOLIDAY HITS
00311329 Book/CD Pack......................$14.95

18. WEST SIDE STORY
00130739 Book/Online Audio $14.99

19. TAYLOR SWIFT
00142735 Book/Online Audio $14.99

20. ANDREW LLOYD WEBBER – FAVORITES
00311775 Book/CD Pack......................$14.99

21. GREAT CLASSICAL MELODIES
00311776 Book/CD Pack......................$14.99

22. ANDREW LLOYD WEBBER – HITS
00311785 Book/CD Pack......................$14.99

23. DISNEY CLASSICS
00311836 Book/CD Pack......................$14.99

24. LENNON & McCARTNEY FAVORITES
00311837 Book/CD Pack......................$14.99

26. WICKED
00311882 Book/CD Pack......................$16.99

27. THE SOUND OF MUSIC
00311897 Book/Online Audio...............$14.99

28. CHRISTMAS CAROLS
00311912 Book/CD Pack......................$14.99

29. CHARLIE BROWN CHRISTMAS
00311913 Book/CD Pack......................$14.99

31. STAR WARS
00110283 Book/Online Audio $16.99

32. SONGS FROM FROZEN, TANGLED AND ENCHANTED
00126896 Book/Online Audio $14.99

Disney characters and artwork © Disney Enterprises, Inc.

Prices, contents and availability subject to change without notice.

FOR MORE INFORMATION, SEE YOUR LOCAL MUSIC DEALER, OR WRITE TO:

HAL•LEONARD®
C O R P O R A T I O N
7777 W. BLUEMOUND RD. P.O. BOX 13819 MILWAUKEE, WI 53213

www.halleonard.com

0516